Enjoying Retirement in the UK

Arthur Crandon LL.B. (Hons) M.A.

Enjoying Retirement in the U.K.

Copyright Arthur Crandon 2024

All rights reserved. No part of this book may be reproduced, stored in a retrieval system, or transmitted in any form or by any means—electronic, mechanical, photocopying, recording, or otherwise—without the prior written permission of the publisher, except for brief quotations in critical reviews or articles. This is a work of fiction. Names, characters, places, and incidents are either the product of the author's imagination or used fictitiously. Any resemblance to actual persons, living or dead, events, or locales is entirely coincidental.

ISBN: 9798342835688
Cover design by Lynnie Ceniza
Interior design and formatting by Lynnie Ceniza
Published by Arthur Crandon Publishing
Visit our website: Arthurcrandon.co.uk

DISCLAIMER

The information provided in this book is for general informational purposes only. It does not constitute legal, financial, or professional advice. While every effort has been made to ensure accuracy, the author and publisher assume no responsibility for errors or omissions. Readers should consult with appropriate professionals for specific advice tailored to their individual circumstances.
First Edition: August 2024

Retirement is a wonderful phase of life, and the UK offers a wealth of opportunities to make the most of it. Whether you're looking for adventure, relaxation, or personal growth, here are some ideas to enjoy your retirement in the UK:

CONTENTS

	Acknowledgments	i
1	De-clutter your home	1
2	Explore	7
3	Become a tour guide and stay active	13
4	Volunteer and Work for nature	25
5	Learn a new skill	37
6	Cooking and Joining Clubs	43
7	Travel and Cultiral Events	53
8	Gardening	67
9	Language	73
10	Technical and Memoirs	77

Remember, retirement isn't about slowing down—it's about embracing new adventures and making the most of every day. Enjoy this vibrant chapter of your life!

1 DECLUTTER YOUR HOME

Decluttering your home during retirement is like opening the windows to let in fresh air—it clears physical space and rejuvenates your mind. Let's dive into why this is a valuable step and how to approach it:

1. ****Why Declutter?**:

    - **Physical Liberation**: Over the years, we accumulate belongings—some cherished, others forgotten. Decluttering frees you from the weight of unnecessary possessions. It's like shedding layers of old skin.

- **Mental Clarity**: A cluttered environment can lead to mental clutter. When you declutter, you create space for clarity, creativity, and peace of mind.

2. ****Where to Begin?**:

    - **Cupboards and Closets**: Start with your cupboards, wardrobes, and drawers. These are treasure troves of forgotten items.

    - **One Area at a Time**: Don't overwhelm yourself. Pick one area—a closet or a specific room—and focus on it.

3. **The Process**:

    - **Sort**: Take everything out. Yes, everything! Sort items into categories: keep, donate, sell, or discard.

    - **Rediscover Treasures**: As you sift through, you'll find forgotten treasures—a childhood photo, a handwritten letter, or a memento from a special trip. Cherish these moments.

- **The 80/20 Rule**: Apply the Pareto Principle. You likely use 20% of your belongings 80% of the time. Keep what truly adds value to your life.

4. **Donate or Sell**:

    - **Donate**: Items in good condition can find new homes. Consider local charities, shelters, or thrift stores. Your old coat might keep someone warm.

    - **Sell**: If you have valuable items, sell them online or at a local market. Use the proceeds for something meaningful.

    - **Sentimental Items**:

        Choose Wisely: Sentimental items hold memories. Keep those that truly evoke joy or have deep significance.

- **Digitize**: Old photos, letters, and documents can be digitized. Preserve the memories without cluttering physical space.

5. **Minimalism and Mindfulness**:

    - **Minimalist Approach**: Embrace minimalism. Ask yourself, "Does this item enhance my life?" If not, let it go.

    - **Mindful Consumption**: Going forward, be mindful of what you bring into your home. Avoid impulsive purchases.

6. **Embrace the Liberation**:

    - **Celebrate**: As you declutter, celebrate each bag of donations or each organized shelf. Acknowledge the progress.

    - **Maintenance**: Regularly revisit your spaces. Prevent clutter from creeping back in.

Remember, decluttering isn't just about physical objects; it's about creating a harmonious environment that supports your well-being. Enjoy the process.

2 EXPLORE

Exploring your local area during retirement is like opening a treasure chest—you'll find unexpected gems right in your backyard. Let's dive into why this approach is so rewarding and how to make the most of it:

1. **The Beauty of Nearby Adventures**:

    - **Hidden Treasures**: Often, we overlook what's close by because we're drawn to far-flung destinations. But within an hour's drive, there's magic waiting—a quaint village, a historic site, or a serene park.

- **Fresh Perspective**: When you explore locally, you see your surroundings with fresh eyes. Suddenly, that park you've passed a hundred times becomes a place of wonder.

2. **Day Trips and Mini-Adventures**:

    - **Nearby Towns**: Research nearby towns or villages. Each has its own character, history, and charm. Visit their markets, cafés, and local landmarks.

    - **Historical Sites**: Explore local castles, old churches, or ancient ruins. Imagine the stories embedded in their stones.

    - **Nature Escapes**: Seek out local parks, nature reserves, or botanical gardens. Take leisurely walks, breathe in the fresh air, and listen to birdsong.

3. **Walking Trails and Scenic Routes**:

    o **Walking Trails**: Lace up your comfortable shoes and hit the trails. Whether it's along a river, through a forest, or across rolling hills, walking connects you to the land.

    o **Coastal Paths**: If you're near the coast, follow coastal paths. Feel the sea breeze, watch waves crash against cliffs, and spot seabirds.

    o **Scenic Drives**: Hop in your car and drive along scenic routes. Stop at viewpoints, snap photos, and enjoy the changing landscapes.

4. **Local Events and Festivals**:

    o **Community Spirit**: Attend local events—farmers' markets, craft fairs, or village festivals. You'll meet friendly faces and experience the community spirit.

- **Seasonal Delights**: From apple picking in autumn to summer garden tours, each season brings unique activities.

5. **Food Adventures**:

    - **Farm Shops and Food Trails**: Explore farm shops selling fresh produce. Follow food trails—visit local dairies, bakeries, and vineyards.

    - **Hidden Cafés and Tearooms**: Seek out charming cafés tucked away on side streets. Sip your coffee or tea while watching the world go by.

6. **Photography Expeditions**:

    - **Capture Moments**: Take your camera or smartphone and capture the essence of your local area. Photograph sunsets, quirky signs, and friendly dogs you meet along the way.

- **Create a Local Photo Diary**: Compile your photos into a visual diary. Share it with friends and family—it's a unique way to document your retirement adventures.

7. **Connect with Locals**:

    - **Strike Up Conversations**: Locals often have fascinating stories. Chat with the owner of the corner shop or the person tending their garden.

    - **Learn Local Lore**: Ask about local legends, historical events, or famous residents. You'll gain insights beyond guidebooks.

Remember, exploring nearby isn't settling; it's savoring the richness of your own patch of Earth. So, put on your explorer's hat, and let curiosity be your compass!

3 STAY ACTIVE – BECOME A TOUR GUIDE

Becoming a tour guide during retirement is like opening a door to a fascinating world—one where you get to share your passion for history, culture, and hidden stories with eager listeners. Let's explore this opportunity further:

1. **Why Become a Tour Guide?**:

    - **Pass on Knowledge**: If you're a history buff or simply love learning about your local area, being a tour guide allows you to pass on that knowledge. You become a living encyclopedia, sharing intriguing facts and anecdotes.

- **Connect with People**: As a guide, you'll meet people from all walks of life—locals, tourists, and fellow enthusiasts. It's a chance to connect, exchange stories, and make new friends.

- **Stay Active**: Tour guiding keeps you physically and mentally active. You'll be on your feet, exploring, and engaging with others.

2. **Where Can You Volunteer?**:
3.
- **National Trust**: You mentioned the National Trust, and it's an excellent place to start. They manage historic houses, gardens, and natural landscapes across the UK. Volunteers lead tours, assist visitors, and contribute to conservation efforts.

- **Local Museums and Heritage Sites**: Check if your local museum or heritage center needs guides. Many rely on volunteers to enhance visitor experiences.

- **Historic Buildings**: Castles, stately homes, and old churches often offer guided tours. Research places near you.

4. **Skills and Qualities Needed**:

    - **Enthusiasm**: Passion is contagious. Your love for history or architecture will inspire others.

    - **Good Communication**: Guides need to articulate well, engage their audience, and answer questions.

    - **Flexibility**: Adapt to different groups—children, adults, or international tourists.

- **Patience**: Not everyone absorbs information at the same pace. Be patient and approachable.

5. **Training and Preparation**:

    - **Learn the Material**: Dive deep into the history of the site you'll be guiding. Know the stories, dates, and quirky details.

    - **Practice Tours**: Start by giving tours to friends or family. Get comfortable with your route and narrative.

    - **Public Speaking**: If you're nervous, consider public speaking courses or workshops.

6. **Tailor Your Tours**:

    - **Themes**: Create themed tours—ghost stories, architectural highlights, or famous residents.

- **Interactive Elements**: Engage your audience. Ask questions, show artifacts, or use visual aids.

- **Local Legends**: Share intriguing local legends or mysteries.

7. **Safety and Accessibility**:

    - **Safety First**: Ensure your tours are safe. Watch out for uneven paths, steps, or slippery areas.

    - **Accessibility**: Consider accessibility for all visitors. Can everyone comfortably participate?

8. **Enjoy the Journey**:

    - **Be Curious**: Keep learning. Even as a guide, stay curious about your surroundings.

    - **Feedback**: Listen to feedback. It helps you improve and tailor your tours.

Remember, being a tour guide isn't just about facts; it's about weaving stories that transport people to another time. So put on your metaphorical tricorn hat (or any hat you like), and let the adventure begin!

Staying physically active during retirement is like investing in your well-being account—it pays dividends in health, happiness, and vitality.

Let's explore why staying active matters and how you can make the most of it:

1. **Physical Health Benefits**:

    - **Heart Health**: Regular physical activity lowers the risk of heart disease and stroke. It keeps your cardiovascular system in top shape.

    - **Blood Pressure**: Exercise helps regulate blood pressure, reducing the strain on your heart.

    - **Diabetes Prevention**: Staying active lowers the risk of type 2 diabetes by improving insulin sensitivity.

    - **Weight Management**: Physical activity helps maintain a healthy weight and prevents weight gain.

2. **Strength and Balance**:

   - **Muscle Strength**: Join fitness classes or lift weights to maintain muscle strength. Strong muscles support your joints and overall mobility.

   - **Balance and Coordination**: Activities like yoga or tai chi enhance balance, reducing the risk of falls.

3. **Bone Health**:

   - **Weight-Bearing Exercise**: Walking, dancing, or hiking are weight-bearing activities that strengthen bones. They help prevent osteoporosis.

   - **Vitamin D**: Outdoor activities expose you to sunlight, which aids in vitamin D production and bone health.

4. **Mental Health Benefits**:

    - **Endorphins**: Exercise releases endorphins—the "feel-good" hormones. They boost mood and reduce stress.

    - **Cognitive Function**: Staying active may improve memory, attention, and overall cognitive abilities.

    - **Anxiety and Depression**: Physical activity reduces symptoms of anxiety and depression.

5. **Social Interaction**:

    - **Group Classes**: Join fitness classes or sports clubs. You'll meet like-minded people and build social connections.

    - **Walking Groups**: Find local walking groups. Walking together combines exercise with socializing.

6. **Adapt to Your Preferences**:

    - **Swimming**: Gentle on joints, swimming is excellent for overall fitness.

    - **Cycling**: Explore scenic routes or cycle to nearby places.

    - **Yoga**: Enhance flexibility, balance, and relaxation through yoga or Pilates.

7. **Set Realistic Goals**:

    - **Start Slow**: If you're new to exercise, begin with short walks or gentle stretches.

    - **Gradual Progress**: Increase intensity or duration gradually. Listen to your body.

8. **Enjoy the Outdoors**:

    - **Nature Walks**: Explore local parks, nature reserves, or coastal paths.

- Fresh air and greenery boost well-being.

- **Gardening**: Tending to your garden is both physical activity and a mental escape.

9. **Stay Hydrated and Rested**:

    - **Hydration**: Drink water before, during, and after exercise.

    - **Rest**: Allow your body to recover. Rest days are essential.

10. **Make It Fun**:

    - **Dance**: Put on your favorite music and dance around your living room.

    - **Play with Grandkids**: Active play with grandchildren keeps you moving.

Remember, staying active isn't about rigid routines; it's about finding joy in movement. Whether it's a leisurely stroll or a vigorous workout, every step counts toward a healthier, happier retirement!

4 CHAPTER NAME

Volunteering for wildlife conservation is like stepping into a vibrant ecosystem—a place where you not only contribute to preserving our planet's biodiversity but also experience personal growth and fulfillment. Let's explore the incredible benefits of working with wildlife and how you can get involved:

1. **Making a Tangible Impact:**

    o When you volunteer in wildlife conservation, you actively engage in safeguarding endangered species and their habitats. Whether it's restoring wetlands, planting trees, or monitoring wildlife populations, your contributions directly lead to positive conservation results.

- **Seeing the real impact of your work**—whether it's a thriving butterfly population, a cleaner beach, or a rescued animal—is immensely satisfying and fulfilling.

2. **Learning and Skill Development:**

   - **Volunteering provides a unique learning opportunity.** You'll gain firsthand knowledge about diverse ecosystems, wildlife behavior, and conservation strategies.

   - **Engaging with experts** allows you to expand your skills in areas such as wildlife tracking, data collection, research techniques, and environmental education. These experiences enhance your understanding of the natural world and open doors to future career paths in conservation.

3. **Immersive Nature Experiences:**

   - **Volunteering often occurs in awe-inspiring natural environments.** Whether you're monitoring sea turtles on a remote beach, assisting with bird banding in a forest, or participating in coral reef restoration, these experiences form lasting memories.

   - **You'll closely observe wildlife,** establish a profound bond with the natural world, and cultivate a deep reverence for Earth's delicate ecosystems.

4. **Personal Growth and Well-being:**

   - **Engaging with nature profoundly affects personal growth and well-being.** Science has shown that a

profound human connection to nature lowers stress levels, improves mental health, and enhances overall well-being.
- Volunteering in these natural settings benefits not only the ecosystem but also your spirit. It instills a sense of purpose, fulfillment, and connection beyond your individuality.

5. **Building Connections and Networks:**

   - **Wildlife conservation volunteering connects you with like-minded individuals**—fellow volunteers, researchers, and passionate conservationists. These connections can lead to lifelong friendships and collaborations.

   - **You become part of a global network of people** dedicated to preserving our planet's natural heritage.

6. Raising Environmental Awareness:

- **As a volunteer, you're not just working behind the scenes;** you're an ambassador for conservation. By sharing your experiences and knowledge, you raise awareness in your community.

- **Whether it's leading educational programs for schoolchildren or talking to visitors at a nature reserve,** your passion inspires others to care for the environment.

So, if nature calls to you, answer it by joining wildlife organizations as a volunteer. Whether you're counting butterflies, planting native trees, or assisting with marine cleanups, every action matters. Let's protect our planet—one paw print, feather, or leaf at a time!

Volunteering is like planting seeds of kindness that grow into a beautiful garden of community well-being. Let's explore why volunteering matters and how you can make a meaningful impact:

1. **Why Volunteer?:**

    - **Sense of Purpose:** Volunteering provides a sense of purpose beyond our individual lives. It connects us to something greater—whether it's supporting vulnerable populations, preserving the environment, or promoting education.

    - **Community Bond:** When you volunteer, you become part of a larger community. You contribute to its resilience, growth, and shared values.

    - **Personal Growth:** Volunteering challenges you, teaches empathy, and broadens your perspective. It's a journey of self-discovery.

2. **Where Can You Volunteer?:**

    o **Local Charities:** These organizations address various needs—food insecurity, homelessness, healthcare access, and more. Volunteer at food banks, shelters, or community clinics.

    o **Schools: Schools often welcome volunteers** for tutoring, mentoring, or assisting with extracurricular activities. Your skills can inspire young minds.

    o **Community Centers:** These hubs offer diverse programs—youth clubs, senior activities, fitness classes, and cultural events. Get involved!

3. **Benefits of Volunteering:**

    o Social Connection: Volunteering introduces you to like-minded people. You'll form friendships and build a support network.

- **Skill Development:** Use your existing skills or learn new ones. Whether it's organizing events, teaching, or fundraising,

  Volunteering hones your abilities.

- **Self-Esteem Boost**: Knowing you've made a difference boosts self-esteem. It's a win-win—you help others and feel good about yourself.

- **Career Prospects:** Volunteering can enhance your resume. Employers value community involvement and leadership skills.

- **Fun and Fulfillment:**

  Volunteering isn't a chore; it's an opportunity for joy. You'll laugh, learn, and create memories.

4. **Types of Volunteering:**

    - **Regular Commitment:** Choose a cause you're passionate about and commit to volunteering regularly. Consistency matters.

    - **One-Time Events:** Participate in community cleanups, charity runs, or disaster relief efforts.

    - **Skills-Based Volunteering:** Offer your professional skills—graphic design, legal advice, or IT support—to nonprofits.

5. **How to Get Started:**

    - **Research:** Look for local organizations that align with your interests. Visit their websites or contact them directly.

    - **Attend Volunteer Fairs:** Many communities host volunteer fairs where you can explore opportunities.

- **Ask Friends and Neighbors:** They might know of local initiatives seeking volunteers.

6. **Remember:**

    - **Start Small:** Begin with a few hours a week. Gradually increase your commitment if you enjoy it.

    - **Be Reliable:** If you commit to a schedule, honor it. Dependability matters.

    - **Enjoy the Journey:** Volunteering isn't just about giving; it's about receiving—receiving gratitude, smiles, and a sense of purpose.

So, put on your volunteer cape and step into the world of giving. Whether you're teaching literacy, planting trees, or comforting someone in need, your impact ripples far beyond the moment.

5 NEW SKILLS

Retirement is like receiving a blank canvas—you have the opportunity to paint it with vibrant colors, learn new melodies, or cultivate a garden of interests. Let's explore the joy of learning new skills during this chapter of life:

1. **Why Learn New Skills in Retirement?**:

    o **Lifelong Curiosity**: Retirement isn't about slowing down; it's about embracing curiosity. Learning keeps your mind agile and your spirit youthful.

    o **Personal Fulfillment**: Remember that hobby you've always been curious about? Now's the time to dive in!

- Whether it's strumming a guitar or mastering watercolor techniques, the journey itself brings immense satisfaction.

2. **Indoor Hobbies to Explore**:

    - **Playing an Instrument**: Dust off that old guitar or keyboard. Learning to play an instrument opens up a world of melodies and self-expression.

    - **Cooking and Baking**: Experiment with flavors, try international cuisines, and perfect your signature dish.

    - **Writing**: Start a journal, write short stories, or even pen your memoirs. Your life experiences are a treasure trove waiting to be shared.

- **Crafts and Art**: From crocheting to painting, these hobbies engage your creativity. You'll surprise yourself with what you can create.

3. **Outdoor and Active Pursuits**:

    - **Gardening**: Plant flowers, grow vegetables, or create a serene oasis. Gardening combines physical activity with the joy of nurturing life.

    - **Photography**: Capture the beauty around you. Learn about composition, lighting, and storytelling through your lens.

    - **Bird Watching**: Invest in binoculars and a field guide. Discover the fascinating world of feathered friends.

4. **Online Learning and Courses**:

    - **Online Classes**: Explore platforms like Coursera, Udemy, or Khan Academy.

- Learn about history, science, or even astrophysics!

- **Language Learning Apps**: Always wanted to speak French or Japanese? Duolingo and Babbel make it fun.

5. **Community Classes and Workshops**:

    - **Local Art Studios**: Take painting or pottery classes. Unleash your inner artist.

    - **Dance Classes**: Tango, salsa, or ballroom—dance keeps you active and socially connected.

    - **Cooking Workshops**: Learn from chefs or join a wine-tasting class.

6. **Remember**:

    - **Patience**: Learning takes time. Celebrate small victories along the way.

- **No Pressure**: It's not about becoming a virtuoso; it's about enjoying the process.

- **Share with Others**: Invite friends or family to join you. Learning together is delightful.

So, whether you're strumming chords, planting seeds, or writing poetry, embrace the thrill of discovery. Retirement isn't an endpoint; it's a canvas waiting for your masterpiece!

6 COOKING AND JOINING CLUBS

Embarking on a culinary adventure in your kitchen is like setting sail to explore uncharted flavor territories. Whether you're a seasoned home cook or a beginner, experimenting with new recipes brings joy, creativity, and a dash of magic to your meals. Let's dive into the delightful world of cooking and exploring new cuisines:

1. **Why Explore New Recipes?:**
2.
    - **Culinary Curiosity:** Cooking isn't just about sustenance; it's an art form. Trying new recipes allows you to discover diverse flavors, techniques, and cultural traditions.

    - **Expand Your Palate:** Each cuisine has its unique palette of spices, herbs, and ingredients. By exploring different culinary traditions, you'll broaden your taste horizons.

    - **Connect with Others:** Sharing a meal from another culture fosters understanding and appreciation. Food transcends borders—it's a universal language.

3. **Getting Started:**

    - **Choose a Cuisine:** Start by selecting a cuisine that intrigues you. It could be Thai, Moroccan, Indian, or Peruvian—the options are endless.

- **Research:** Dive into cookbooks, food blogs, or cooking shows. Learn about staple ingredients, flavor profiles, and traditional dishes.

4. **Equip Your Kitchen:**

    - **Basic Tools:** Ensure you have essential kitchen tools—a sharp knife, cutting board, pots, pans, and measuring cups.

    - **Spices and Herbs:** Stock up on spices and herbs specific to the cuisine you're exploring. They're the heart of flavor.

5. **Start Simple:**

    - **Beginner-Friendly Recipes:** Look for straightforward recipes. Master a classic dish before tackling complex ones.

    - **Comfort Zone**: If you love Italian food, try making homemade pasta or risotto. If you're curious about Korean cuisine, start with bibimbap or kimchi.

6. **Ingredient Exploration:**

    - **Visit Ethnic Markets:** Explore local ethnic markets or specialty stores. Discover unique ingredients—tamarind paste, miso, saffron, or garam masala.
    - Fresh Produce: Experiment with seasonal fruits and vegetables. Try jicama, plantains, or kohlrabi.

7. **Flavor Fusion:**

    - **Blend Cultures:** Don't be afraid to mix and match. Food fusion is exciting! Combine elements from different cuisines—for example, Korean tacos or Thai-inspired pizza.

    - **Spice Blends:** Create your spice blends. Mix cumin, coriander, and turmeric for an Indian-inspired seasoning.

8. **Learn Techniques:**

    - **Stir-Frying:** Master the art of stir-frying (Chinese, Thai, or Vietnamese). It's quick, vibrant, and full of fresh veggies.
    - Slow Cooking: Explore stews, tagines, or curries. Slow-cooked dishes develop rich flavors.

9. **Document Your Journey:**

    - **Cooking Journal:** Keep a journal of your experiments. Note what worked, what surprised you, and any adjustments you made.
    - Food Photos: Capture your creations. Share them with friends or on social media.

10. **Invite Friends and Family:**

    - **Cook Together:** Host themed dinner nights. Invite loved ones to join you in exploring a specific cuisine.

- **Potluck Parties:** Have friends bring dishes from their favorite cuisines. It's a delicious cultural exchange.

11. **Embrace Mistakes:**

    - **Trial and Error:** Not every dish will be perfect. That's okay! Learn from mistakes and adapt.
    - Celebrate Successes: When you nail a recipe, celebrate with a joyful dance or a heartfelt toast.

Remember, cooking is an adventure—a blend of science, art, and love. So tie on your apron, turn up the music, and let your kitchen become a canvas for creativity!

Joining clubs and groups is like stepping into a vibrant tapestry of shared interests, camaraderie, and new adventures. Whether you're passionate about literature, photography, or salsa dancing, these communities offer a delightful blend of connection and growth.

Let's explore why joining clubs and groups is a fantastic idea:

1. **Social Networking Opportunities**:

    - Clubs and groups are lively hubs where people gather around shared passions. Whether it's a book club discussing the latest novel or a hiking group exploring scenic trails, you'll meet like-minded individuals.

    - These gatherings provide a relaxed and friendly setting for social interaction. You'll swap stories, share experiences, and build lasting friendships.

2. **Access to Exclusive Facilities**:

    - Many clubs offer exclusive facilities related to their focus. Imagine joining a photography club with access to a darkroom or a tennis club with well-maintained courts.

    - Clubhouses become cozy meeting spots where members connect over coffee or a game of chess

3. **Health and Well-being Benefits**:

    - **Mental Stimulation**: Engaging in club activities keeps your mind active. Whether you're solving puzzles in a chess club or discussing literature, mental stimulation is vital.

    - **Physical Activity**: Sports clubs, dance groups, or hiking clubs keep you physically active. It's exercise disguised as fun!

4. **Skill Development and Learning**:

    o **Learn from Peers**: Clubs provide a platform for skill exchange. You'll learn from experienced members and share your expertise.

    o **Workshops and Workgroups**: Many clubs organize workshops, guest lectures, or collaborative projects. It's continuous learning in action.

5. **Sense of Belonging**:

    o **Community**: Clubs create a sense of belonging. You're part of something bigger—a tribe that celebrates your interests.

    o **Support System**: When life throws curveballs, your clubmates become your cheerleaders.

6. **Expand Your Horizons**:

    - **Cultural Exchange**: Joining international clubs or language exchange groups exposes you to different cultures and perspectives.

    - **Try New Things**: Ever considered square dancing or urban sketching? Clubs encourage you to step out of your comfort zone.

7. **How to Find Clubs and Groups**:

    - **Meetup.com**: Explore local events, hobby groups, and gatherings. Meetup connects you with people who share your interests.

    - **Local Newspapers and Community Centers**: Check event listings or community boards.

- **Online Searches**: Type "[your interest] clubs near me" into search engines.

Remember, clubs aren't just about the activity; they're about the people. So whether you're discussing plot twists in a book club or capturing sunsets with fellow photographers, enjoy the journey—it's more than a hobby; it's a community!

7 TRAVEL AND CULTURAL EVENTS

Traveling within the UK is like embarking on a treasure hunt—you'll discover historical gems, charming villages, and breathtaking coastal vistas. Whether you're a history enthusiast, a nature lover, or simply seeking new experiences, here's how to make the most of your UK exploration:

1. **Historical Sites and Landmarks**:

    - **Castles**: Wander through ancient castles like Warwick Castle, Edinburgh Castle, or Caernarfon Castle. Feel the weight of history within their stone walls.

    - **Stonehenge**: Marvel at the enigmatic Stonehenge—a prehistoric monument that continues to intrigue visitors.

    - **Roman Baths in Bath**: Immerse yourself in Roman history at the well-preserved baths in the city of Bath.

2. **Coastal Towns and Seaside Escapes**:

    - **Cornwall**: Explore Cornwall's rugged coastline, with picturesque villages like St. Ives and Port Isaac. Don't miss the stunning cliffs of Land's End.

- **Whitby**: Visit the charming town of Whitby, famous for its Gothic abbey ruins and connections to Bram Stoker's "Dracula."

  Brighton: Enjoy the vibrant atmosphere of Brighton—stroll along the iconic pier, explore the Lanes, and dip your toes in the English Channel.

3. **Picturesque Villages**:

    - **Bibury**: Discover the idyllic Cotswold village of Bibury, known for its honey-colored stone cottages and the tranquil River Coln.

    - **Lavenham**: Step back in time in Lavenham, Suffolk. Its medieval timber-framed buildings are straight out of a fairy tale.

    - **Portmeirion**: Visit the whimsical Italianate village of Portmeirion in Wales. It's like stepping into a Mediterranean dream.

4. **House Swaps and Staycations**:

    o **House Swaps**: Inspired by "The Holiday"? House swapping is a fantastic way to experience a new location without breaking the bank. You exchange your home with someone else's, immersing yourself in their neighborhood and daily life.

    o **Staycations**: Opt for staycations—vacations within your own country. Book a cozy cottage, a seaside apartment, or a countryside retreat. Enjoy lazy mornings, explore nearby trails, and savor local cuisine.

5. **Travel Tips**:

    o **Plan Ahead**: Research the areas you want to visit. Check opening hours, entry fees, and any COVID-related guidelines.

- **Public Transport**: Consider trains or buses for longer journeys. The UK has an extensive rail network connecting cities and scenic routes.

- **Local Cuisine**: Try regional specialties—Cornish pasties, Yorkshire puddings, or Scottish haggis.

Remember, the UK is a patchwork of history, culture, and natural beauty. Whether you're sipping tea in a tearoom or hiking along coastal cliffs, each experience adds a brushstroke to your travel canvas. Bon voyage!

Attending cultural events is like stepping into a kaleidoscope of creativity, where art, music, and human expression converge. Whether you're drawn to the hallowed halls of museums, the vibrant energy of live performances, or the communal spirit of festivals, the UK offers a rich tapestry of cultural experiences.

Let's explore why attending these events is a delightful journey:

1. **Museums and Art Galleries**:

   - **Time Travel**: Museums are portals to the past. Wander through the British Museum, where ancient artifacts whisper tales of civilizations long gone. Or explore the Tate Modern, where contemporary art challenges your perspective.

   - **Masterpieces**: Stand before iconic paintings—the enigmatic smile of the Mona Lisa at the Louvre or Turner's seascapes at the National Gallery.

- Each stroke carries centuries of human emotion.

2. **Theatrical Magic**:

    - **West End Shows**: London's West End is a theatrical wonderland. From Shakespearean tragedies to toe-tapping musicals, immerse yourself in the magic of live performances.

    - **Local Theaters**: Don't overlook local theaters. Intimate venues often host groundbreaking plays and emerging talent.

3. **Concerts and Music Festivals**:

    - **Royal Albert Hall**: Attend a classical concert at the Royal Albert Hall—an architectural gem. Let the symphony wash over you.

- **Glastonbury**: If you're a music lover, Glastonbury Festival is a pilgrimage. Mud, music, and unforgettable moments await.

4. **Unique Cultural Celebrations**:

    - **Edinburgh Fringe Festival**: In August, Edinburgh transforms into an artistic playground. Comedy, theatre, and street performances fill every nook. It's chaos and brilliance combined.

    - **Notting Hill Carnival**: Join the rhythm of steel drums and colorful costumes at this Caribbean-inspired street festival. Dance, feast, and celebrate diversity.

5. **Literary Gatherings**:

    - **Hay Festival**: Nestled in the Welsh town of Hay-on-Wye, this literary extravaganza brings together authors, poets, and thinkers.

- Dive into discussions and book signings.

- **Bookshops**: Explore independent bookshops—each one a treasure trove of stories waiting to be discovered.

6. **Film Festivals**:

    - **BFI London Film Festival**: Catch premieres, documentaries, and hidden gems. Rub shoulders with filmmakers and cinephiles.

    - **Local Screenings**: Check out indie cinemas—they often screen thought-provoking films you won't find elsewhere.

7. **Art Exhibitions**:

    - **Towner Art Gallery**: Visit the Towner Art Gallery in Eastbourne. It's a blend of contemporary art and historical pieces, set against the stunning South Downs.

    -

- **Street Art**: Wander through Shoreditch in London or the streets of Bristol. Graffiti and murals tell stories of rebellion and creativity.

Remember, cultural events aren't just about passive observation; they're invitations to engage, question, and feel. So put on your cultural explorer hat, and let the canvas of creativity unfold before you!

8 GARDENING

Gardening is like whispering secrets to the earth and watching them bloom into life. Whether you're tending to a tiny balcony garden or embracing the expanse of a backyard oasis, the rewards are abundant.

Let's dig into the fertile soil of gardening and explore why it's a delightful journey for both body and soul:

1. **Therapeutic Touch of Soil:**

    o **Grounding:** When your hands touch soil, you connect with the heartbeat of the Earth. Gardening grounds you—literally and metaphorically.

    o **Stress Relief:** Weeding, planting, and nurturing plants provide a soothing rhythm. It's like a massage for your mind.

2. **Physical Activity and Vitality:**

    o **Natural Exercise:** Gardening is a workout in disguise. Digging, lifting pots, and bending—your muscles get a gentle but effective workout.

    o **Sun-Kissed Vitamin D**: Spending time outdoors exposes you to sunlight, boosting your vitamin D levels. Strong bones and a happy mood—what a combo!

3. **Harvest of Joy:**

    o **Homegrown Bounty:** Imagine plucking sun-warmed tomatoes or fragrant basil from your garden. The taste? Pure magic.

    o **Floral Symphony:** Flowers nod in gratitude. Their colors and fragrances dance to the rhythm of your care.

4. **Small Spaces, Big Dreams:**

    o **Balcony Bliss:** Even a tiny balcony can host herbs, succulents, or cherry tomatoes. Vertical planters maximize space.

    o **Windowsill Wonders:** Microgreens thrive on sunny windowsills. Harvest nutrient-packed greens in weeks.

5. **Garden Wisdom for Beginners:**

    o **Start Small:** Better a proud herb pot than a frustrated jungle.

Choose a manageable area.

- Sunlight Savvy: Observe where sunlight kisses your space. Most veggies crave 6-8 hours of sun.

- Container Magic: Use pots, raised beds, or hanging baskets. Soil, seeds, and love—your recipe for growth.

- Herb Haven: Basil, mint, and chives adore windowsills. Fresh herbs elevate your cooking.

6. **Garden Whispers:**

- **Talk to Your Plants:** They're great listeners. Share your dreams, and they'll bloom in agreement.

- **Watch Miracles Unfold:** From seed to sprout, witness life's magic. Each leaf unfurls with purpose.

Remember, gardening isn't just about plants; it's about nurturing your own well-being. So grab a trowel, dance with the seasons, and let your garden be a canvas of joy!

9 LANGUAGE

Learning a new language during retirement is like planting a seed that blossoms into a bouquet of cultural understanding and mental agility. Whether you dream of ordering croissants in Parisian cafés or conversing with locals in Barcelona, language learning offers a delightful journey. Here's why it's a fantastic endeavor and some practical steps to get started:

1. **Why Learn a Language in Retirement?**:

    o **Brain Boost**: Learning a language stimulates your brain. It builds new neural connections, improves memory, and enhances concentration.

    o **Cultural Exploration**: Speaking a new language opens doors to different cultures, traditions, and perspectives. It's like having a backstage pass to the world.

    o **Travel Companion**: Imagine confidently navigating foreign streets, reading menus, and making friends wherever you go.

2. **Practical Tips for Language Learning**:

    o **Choose Your Language**: French, Spanish, Italian, Mandarin—pick one that excites you. Consider your travel aspirations or personal interests.

- **Apps and Websites**:

  - **Duolingo**: A free app that gamifies language learning. Perfect for beginners and beyond.

  - **Rosetta Stone**: Great for self-paced learning. It's like having a personal tutor.

  - **Memrise**: Interactive and effective for vocabulary building.

  - **Transparent Language Online**: Offers a wide range of languages and cultural insights.

- **Set Realistic Goals**: Decide how much time you'll dedicate each day. Consistency matters more than cramming.

- **Practice Speaking**: Find language exchange partners or join conversation groups.

- Speaking accelerates learning.

- **Immerse Yourself**: Watch movies, listen to music, and read books in your chosen language.

- **Be Patient and Persistent**: Learning a language is like tending a garden. Small efforts yield beautiful blooms.

Remember, language learning isn't just about words; it's about connecting hearts across borders. So grab your virtual passport, and let the adventure begin!

10 TECHNOLOGY AND MEMOIRS

Embracing technology during retirement is like discovering a treasure trove of connections, entertainment, and convenience. Let's explore how you can dive into the digital world and stay connected with loved ones.

1. **Social Media: Connecting Across Miles**

    - **What Is Social Media?**: Social media platforms are like virtual meeting places where people share, connect, and engage. Think of them as digital coffee shops or community centers.

- **Popular Platforms for Seniors**:

  - **Facebook**: A versatile platform for connecting with family, friends, and interest groups.

  - **YouTube**: Explore videos on any topic—from cooking to travel to music.

  - **Instagram**: Share photos and short videos with a visual flair.

  - **LinkedIn**: Ideal for professional networking and staying updated on industry news.

  - **Twitter**: Follow news, trends, and favorite personalities in bite-sized updates.

2. **Video Calls: Faces Across Screens**

    o **FaceTime (Apple Devices)**: If you have an iPhone, iPad, or Mac, FaceTime lets you video chat seamlessly with other Apple users.

    o **Google Duo**: Simple and user-friendly, it works on both Android and iOS devices.

    o **Zoom**: Widely used for group video calls, virtual events, and meetings.

    o **Skype**: Connect with loved ones worldwide—great for international calls.

3. **Online Platforms: Learning and Exploring**

    o **Online Classes**: Explore platforms like Senior Planet or take courses on topics that interest you.

- **Social Media Tutorials**: Learn how to set up profiles, navigate feeds, and connect with others.

- **Apps and Websites**: Install apps for news, weather, hobbies, and more.

Remember, technology isn't about mastering every gadget; it's about using tools that enhance your life. So grab your digital compass, and let's explore this exciting terrain together!

Writing your memoirs is like weaving a tapestry of memories—a way to preserve your life experiences, share wisdom, and leave a lasting legacy. Whether you choose to keep it within your family circle or consider publishing, the journey of memoir writing is both therapeutic and transformative.

Let's explore why it's worth embarking on this literary adventure:

1. **The healing power of memoirs**:

    o **Self-reflection**: writing your life story allows you to revisit moments—both joyful and challenging. It's a form of self-reflection that can bring clarity and healing.

    o **Strength in vulnerability**: even painful memories gain strength when shared. By revisiting them, you acknowledge your resilience and growth.

2. **Passing down wisdom**:

    o **Life lessons**: your memoirs are a treasure trove of lessons learned. Whether it's overcoming adversity, finding love, or navigating career choices, your experiences can guide others.

    o **Generational connection**: imagine your descendants reading your memoirs—a direct link to their roots and heritage.

3. **Therapeutic benefits**:

    o **Emotional catharsis**: writing about difficult moments can be cathartic. It's like releasing emotional baggage.

    o **processing trauma**: research shows that writing about upsetting memories can be as effective as therapy for conditions like post-traumatic stress disorder.

4. **Choosing your path to publication**:

   o **Traditional publishing**:

      - Write a compelling book proposal.
      - Pitch your memoir to literary agents.
      - If accepted, the agent will help you secure a publishing deal.

   o **Self-publishing**:

      - Take control of the process.
      - Design your book cover.
      - Choose distribution channels (e.g., amazon, local bookstores).
      - Market your memoir directly to your audience.

5. **Tips for starting your memoir**:

    o **Begin with memories**: reflect on significant life events. Consider your childhood home, pivotal relationships, or transformative moments.

    o **Photo albums**: flip through old photo albums. Each picture holds a story waiting to be told.

    o **Writing prompts**: use prompts like "my fondest memory of..." or "the time i was happiest/scared was..."

    o **Themes**: focus on specific themes—love, resilience, adventure, or personal growth.

Remember, your memoirs are more than words on paper; they're a bridge between generations. So pick up your pen or open your laptop, and let your life story unfold

ABOUT THE AUTHOR

Arthur Crandon is a retired lawyer and a prolific writer. He is British and grew up in a rural community in Somerset. He has lived in England, Wales, Hong Kong and the Philippines and now spends most of his time in the Philippines with his Visayan wife and their son.

He loves to hear from anyone who has anything to do with the Philippines – you can email him anytime on:

ac@arthurcrandon.co.uk

www.ingramcontent.com/pod-product-compliance
Lightning Source LLC
Chambersburg PA
CBHW070342230526
45471CB00006B/2416